LOUVRE

LOUVRE

Pierre Quoniam

Inspecteur général
honoraire des musées de France

Réunion
des Musées
Nationaux

Contents

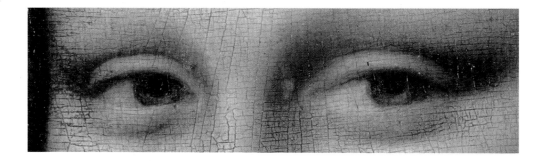

Design: *Cpapus 89.*

ISBN: 2-7118-3000-4 (French edition)
ISBN: 2-7118-3001-2 (English edition)

© Editions de la Réunion des musées nationaux, 1993
49, rue Etienne-Marcel, 75001 Paris

Entresol

/ escalators

↗ stairs

• toilets

- Oriental Antiquities,
  Islamic Art
- Egyptian Antiquities
- Greek, Etruscan
  and Roman Antiquities
- Objets d'Art
- Sculpture
- Prints and Drawings
- Paintings

- Medieval Louvre

RICHELIEU

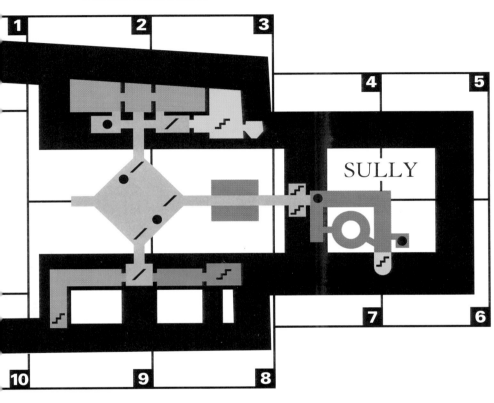

1 **2** **3**

4 **5**

SULLY

7 **6**

10 **9** **8**

DENON

Ground floor

/ escalators
⌐ stairs
• toilets

▨ Oriental Antiquities,
Islamic Art
▨ Egyptian Antiquities
▨ Greek, Etruscan
and Roman Antiquities
▨ Objets d'Art
▨ Sculpture
▨ Prints and Drawings
▨ Paintings

▨ Medieval Louvre

RICHELIEU

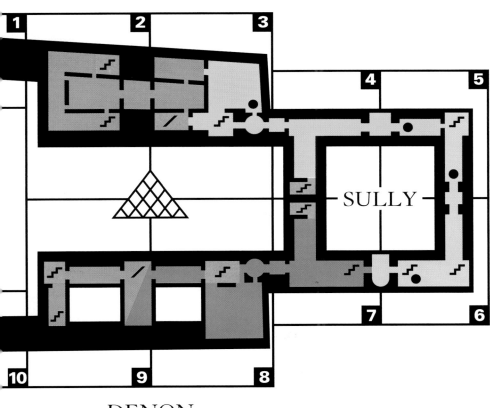

SULLY

DENON

First floor

/ escalators
↳ stairs
• toilets

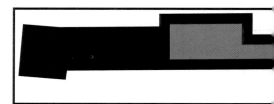

Oriental Antiquities,
Islamic Art
Egyptian Antiquities
Greek, Etruscan
and Roman Antiquities
Objets d'Art
Sculpture
Prints and Drawings
Paintings

Medieval Louvre

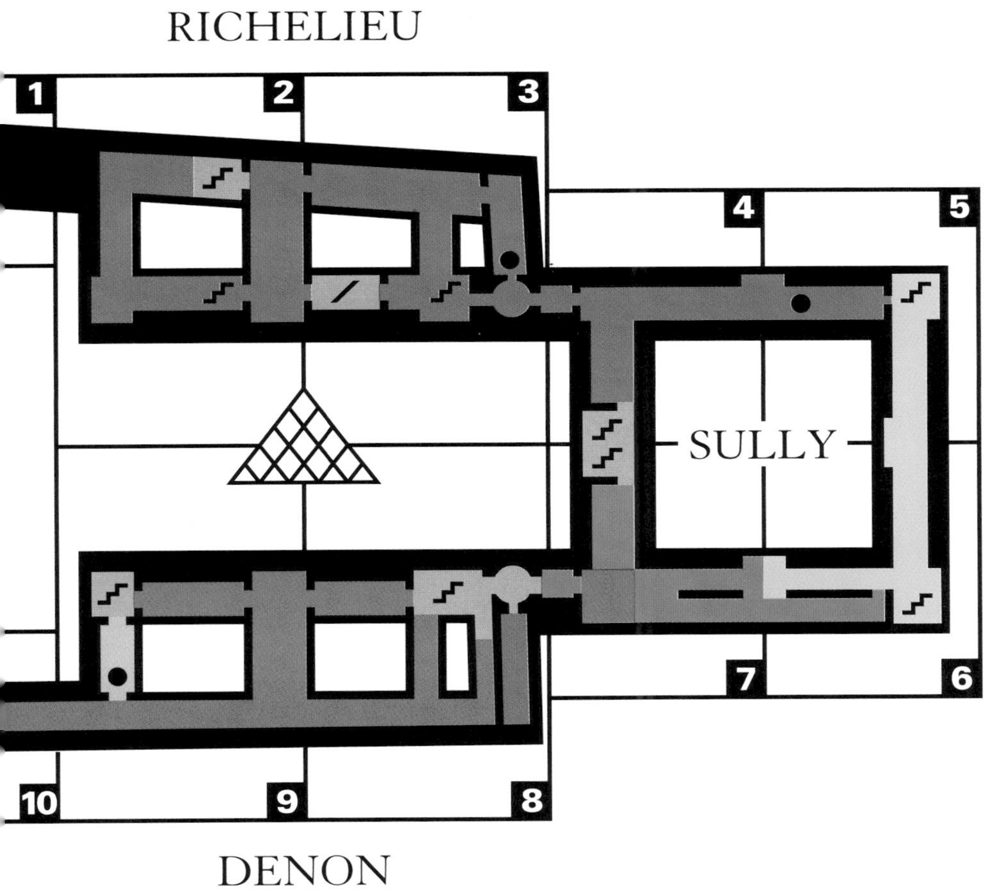

RICHELIEU

1   **2**   **3**

4   **5**

SULLY

10   **9**   **8**

7   **6**

DENON

Second floor

■ **Paintings**

French Paintings :
XIVth-XVIIth centuries   **3 4 5**
XVIIIth-XIXth centuries   **5 6 7**

Information Centre   **3**

Paintings, Northern Schools :
Holland, Flanders,   **2 3**
Germany

■ **Prints and Drawings**

French School :
XVIIth century   **4**
XVIIIth century   **5 6**

Northern Schools   **3**

╱ escalators
♪ stairs
● toilets

Oriental Antiquities,
Islamic Art
Egyptian Antiquities
Greek, Etruscan
and Roman Antiquities
Objets d'Art
Sculpture
Prints and Drawings
Paintings

Medieval Louvre

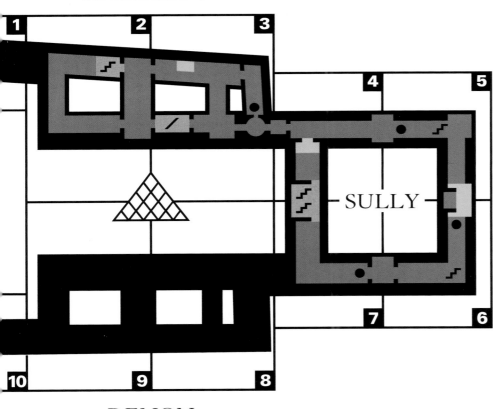

RICHELIEU

DENON

SULLY

1 2 3 4 5 6 7 8 9 10

Preface

In memory of Pierre Quoniam

"Quoniam's!" All the curators of the Louvre, whether young or not-so-young, know how useful this museum guide is; updated at each new edition, it gets bigger and better all the time. It is named after the former director of the museum, who devoted so much time and energy to it – Pierre Quoniam. The guide offers a clear cogent presentation of the collections in the seven departments of the Louvre museum.

The three departments of antiquities show how the great civilisations of the Middle East, Egypt and the Mediterranean emerged and evolved, from the third millenium B.C. until the first centuries of the Christian era. The four "modern" departments trace the development of European art from the Early Middle Ages to the 19th century, presenting sculpture, decorative arts, painting and graphic arts.

Is the Louvre's version of the history of art complete, and if so, is it entirely impartial? Of course not. To begin with, some aspects of the subject are treated in other national museums. Late 19th- and 20th-century art is found at the Musée d'Orsay and at the Musée National d'Art Moderne, while Eastern and Far Eastern art belong to the Musée des Arts Asiatiques-Guimet, and African and Pacific art fall within the domain of the Musée National des Arts d'Afrique et d'Océanie.

It would be pointless to try and draw up a list of the world's top museums: what each one has to offer is inextricably linked to the circumstances in which its collections were assembled and the vicissitudes of its history. The Louvre's particular good fortune is that it may exhibit both a royal gallery inherited from France's ancien régime (like the great museums of Florence, Madrid and Vienna) and collections gradually acquired in the 19th and 20th centuries (like those of Berlin, London and New York) through a consistent purchasing policy and, of course, generous private donations.

One of the priceless amenities distinguishing the Louvre from its rivals is the backdrop it provides to its collections. There was always the palatial architecture, which spans three hundred years from the 16th to the 19th century, and its extraordinary site in the heart of the city. But the "Grand Louvre" project has widened the museum's perspective even further, with a view to both the past and the present. The excavation of the *Cour Carrée* (Square Courtyard) brought to light the monumental moat belonging to the original château of Philippe Auguste and Charles V, which epitomized the power of the monarchy; while the Napoleon Hall and courtyard fronted by I.M. Pei's pyramid, followed by the conversion of the former Ministry of Finance into museum space, has secured a place for the Louvre in the history of contemporary architecture.

With the opening of the Richelieu Wing and – more recently – the rooms devoted to foreign sculpture from the German Middle Ages to Canova, can we say that the Louvre's vast renovation programme has now been completed? Given the formidable task still facing the curators of the three archaeological departments, as well as those of Paintings, Objets d'Arts and Graphic Arts, the answer to that question can only be no. We invite visitors to judge what has already been achieved and to take stock of what remains to be done (and we would like to apologise for any inconvenience this may cause). What we are trying to do is to make their visits easier and more enjoyable. So may this sense of delectation so dear to Poussin be their guide!

Pierre Rosenberg
Président and Director of the Louvre Museum

Hubert ROBERT
**Projet for alterations
to the Great Gallery of the Louvre
in 1796** *(central area)*

The Louvre Palace and Museum

The Louvre was originally a medieval fortress, built in 1200 during Philippe Auguste's reign, on a location at which Paris's defenses were the weakest. The site was called Lupara, which became Louvre in French. This location corresponds to the present site of the southwest quarter of the Square Courtyard, where a quantity of impressive remains, unearthed between 1984 and 1985, are now on view in the **basement 1**. When the structure ceased to serve as a defense post, Charles V (1364-1380) enlarged it and made it into a royal residence **2**. However, its new function soon came to an end: the vicissitudes of the Hundred Years' War, and eventually the attraction of the Loire valley diverted the sovereign's attention from their capital city for over one and a half centuries.

After their return to Paris, the early fortified castle vanished. François I had its imposing keep demolished in 1527, and, in 1546, decided to replace the rest by a Renaissance style building. This undertaking was assigned to the architect Pierre Lescot, who completed it under the last Valois kings and is assumed to have drafted the plans of the new palace **3**. Whatever the case, the work was carried on over the ensuing reigns and centuries in the same spirit of classical regularity.

Catherine de' Medici commissioned Philibert Delorme and Jean Bulland to construct two galleries about 500 meters to the west, on a location known as the *Tuileries*, designed to connect the partially transformed Louvre with the palace built at the same period. These are the *Small Gallery* and the *Great Gallery*,

the latter also being known as the "Riverside Gallery", associated with Henri IV (1589-1610). In the 17th century, under Louis XIII and later Louis XIV, the other buildings surrounding the present *Square Courtyard* were erected by Lemercier and Le Vau. They are flanked on the east by **Perrault's colonnade 4**.

In the early 19th century, under Napoleon I, Percier and Fontaine began the construction of the north wing, symmetrical with the Great Gallery, while also completing the quadrilateral buildings and their decoration. Half a century later, Napoleon III had Visconti and Lefuel construct the buildings bordering the **Napoleon courtyard 5** on the north and south, designed to complete the enclosure of the space between the early Louvre and the Tuileries. However, the Tuileries palace was burned to the ground in 1871, and the unity of the huge palatial ensemble was destroyed on the west. The only buildings that were restored were the two corner pavilions-the *pavillon de Marsan* (along the rue de Rivoli) and the *pavillon de Flore* (along the Seine), together with their immediately adjoining prolongations.

Although the Louvre Museum did not come into being until the end of the 18th century, during the French Revolution, the idea for it had been launched forty years earlier. In a pamphlet decrying the secrecy of the royal collections, Lafont de Saint-Yenne had recommended that the latter be displayed to the public in the palace's Great Gallery.
In response to this recommendation, which was echoed by other writers and

1 Vestiges of the medieval château
In the foreground: the tower on the north-east corner, known as the "Tour de la Taillerie"

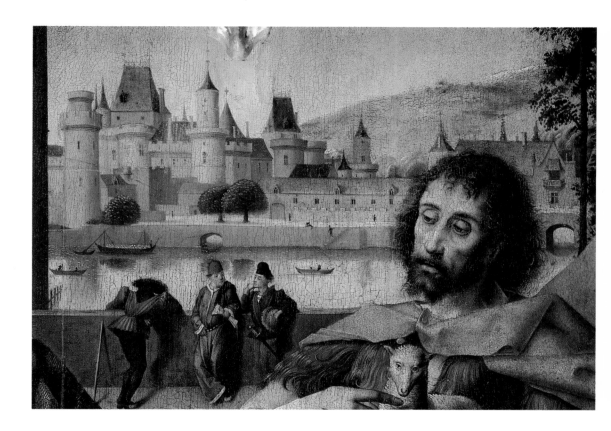

2 The medieval Louvre: detail of the "Retable of the Paris Parliament"
Mid-15th century

philosophers, notably by Diderot in his *Encyclopédie* (in the article entitled "*Le Louvre*", 1765), an initial project was unsuccessfully submitted to Louis XV by the Marquis de Marigny, director of buildings. The idea was taken up again under Louis XVI and studied attentively by Count d'Angiviller, Marigny's successor. However, it came to naught because of financial difficulties and political events.

The Convention deserves the credit for making this dream come true after the fall of the monarchy. The Central Museum of the Arts was set up by decree on July 27th, 1793, and was inaugurated on August 10th of that year. However, this opening proved to be partial and temporary. The Great Gallery, where the paintings were exhibited, and the ground floor of the Small Gallery devoted to antiquities were gradually made ready throughout the Revolution and the First Empire, with major work actively proceeding after 1802, when Vivant Denon became the museum's managing director. The establishment was continuously enriched with objects brought back from the wars; and it was named the Napoleonic Museum in 1803, when it presented what was probably the most splendid collection of masterpieces of all time.

This collection was dispersed in 1815 by the restitutions imposed by the allies after Napoleon's downfall. However the Louvre collections were again rapidly increased under the Restoration and the July Monarchy, notably through the transfer to the palace of some of the sculptures from the Museum of French Monuments, closed in 1817, and through the continuous development of the departments of Greek, Roman, Egyptian and Oriental antiquities. The museum thus gradually spread out into the four wings of the Square Courtyard. Under the Second Empire, a further

³ Pierre Lescot's façade for the Square Courtyard in 1553
Engraving by Jacques Ier Androuet du Cerceau
Bibliothèque nationale

⁴ The Louvre Palace: Perrault's colonnade

wing was constructed with the Denon pavilion at its centre. At the same time, three more buildings were added to link this new wing with the Great Gallery; together, the new display rooms formed a more viable circuit for visitors, better adapted to the quantity and variety of works exhibited. Subsequently, the museum has had to keep abreast with developments in museology, art history and archeology, not to mention the steady expansion both of its collections, and of the crowds who come to see them. Today, it is estimated that up to five million people pass through the Louvre every year. The buildings have undergone an almost continuous process of change right up to the present time, culminating with the opening of the Flore Pavilion in 1968, and with a decision by the President of the Republic in September 1981 to restore to the museum a section of the palace occupied by the Ministry of Finance.

This decision has been one of enormous importance, for two reasons. First, it has provided new exhibition space enabling a complete reorganization of the collections; and second, it holds out the possibility of a far more compact museum, easier to find one's way around than the present seven hundred metre labyrinth extending between the Flore Pavilion and the Colonnade. In 1989, the Louvre was finally given the main entrance it had lacked for over three hundred years, complete with reception facilities at the basement level. These facilities were designed by the architect I.M. Pei, who is also responsible for the glass pyramid 6 which crowns them.

During construction work, archeological excavation brought to light the vestiges of Philippe Auguste and Charles v's medieval Louvre. The former Ministry of Finance in the Richelieu Wing, to the north, was entirely refitted in 1993, revealing both its historic apartments,

sumptuously decorated under Napoleon III, and its rooms devoted to French and Nordic Painting (2nd floor), Decorative Arts (1st floor), Oriental and Islamic Antiquities (ground floor and mezzanine), together with French Sculpture (ground floor) which is also to be found under glass in the courtyards.

5 The Napoleon courtyard during the Second Empire
Photo by Ed. Baldus, 1857

Musée d'Orsay

6 I.M. Pei's Pyramid

Oriental Antiquities

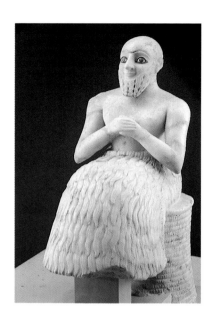

The Oriental Antiquities department, housed on the ground floor, in the eastern part of the Richelieu Wing, and on the northern – soon to be reorganized – side and western half of the Square Courtyard, presents a virtually complete panorama of ancient Near Eastern civilizations. This department was created in 1881, and its his-tory is closely linked with the development of archeological research in Mesopotamia, Iran, the Levant, Cyprus and Punic North Africa. It started with Paul Emile Botta's excavations in Khorsabad in 1843 – the objects from which enabled the founding of the Louvre's first "Assyrian Museum" in 1847 – to the contemporary findings of Claude Schaeffer at Ras-Shamra and of André Parrot at Mari, and includes notably the discoveries of the Renan mission to the Lebanon (1860), of the Persian delegation, whose first director, in 1897, was Jacques de Morgan, and of the French archeologists who explored the site of Telloh in Lower Mesopotamia from 1877 to 1933, and brought back the revelation of the Sumerian civilization.

The section devoted to early Mesopotamia, Sumer and Akkad, is especially rich. This period is illustrated by important monuments, such as the *Stele of the Vultures*, erected in 2450 BC by E-annatum, prince of Lagash, in memory of his conquests. An alabaster statuette from Mari, a masterpiece of Sumerian-inspired Mesopotamian art, dates from about 2500 BC. It was dedicated by the intendant **Ebih-il 7** to the goddess Ishtar. The worshipping figure is seated on a wickerwork stool and garbed in a sheepskin skirt. The inlaid eyes impart intense life to the face, and this effect is enhanced by the half-smile that seems to hover on its lips. In the Akkadian era, King **Naram-Sin 8** raised a stele (circa 2270 BC) to commemorate his victory over the barbarians of the Zagros mountains on the borders of Iran. This masterly composition depicts Naram-Sin as a god, striding up a wooded mountainside and trampling his fallen enemies underfoot. Various representations of this prince of Lagash bear witness to the Sumerian renaissance at the end of the third millennium, during the reign of the administrator **Gudea 9**. One of them, in calcite, shows him holding a vase, a divine attribute, from which fish-filled, lifegiving water is flowing forth.

One object that is both a work of art and a historical document stands out in this department-and in the whole Louvre Museum-testifying more eloquently than anything else to the grandeur of the first Babylonian kingdom.

This is the **Code of King Hammurabi 10** (1792-1750 BC), discovered in 1901 at Susa, where it had been brought as booty during the 12th century BC. This conical stele of basalt is 2.25 meters high and covered with cuneiform script, in the Akkadian language. It constitutes not so much a "code" as it does a compendium of common law, of exemplary statements dictated by the king "so that his country might learn firm discipline and proper conduct". At the top, a majestic scene shows Hammurabi standing in an attitude of prayer before Shamash, god of the sun and of justice.

The vestiges that testify to Assyrian might from the 9th to the 7th century BC possess a dramatic quality. Great reliefs-decorative elements from the palaces of

7 Ebih-il, intendant of Mari
Circa 2500 BC
Richelieu 3, Ground Floor

8 Stele of Naram-Sin, king of Akkad

Circa 2270 BC

Richelieu 3, Ground Floor

9 Gudea with flowing vase

Circa 2150 BC

Richelieu 3, Ground Floor

25

Nimrud, Nineveh and, especially, Khorsabad-evoke the glorious deeds of the kings who raised these vast buildings, particularly those of **Sargon II 11** (721-705 BC), represented in his duties as the supreme administrator, issuing instructions to his minister. Huge sculptures hint at the immensity of the palace erected by this king at Khorsabad: **Winged bulls with human heads 12**, four meters high, are guardian spirits standing watch over the palace entrances, together with lion-taming giants. This monumental group from now on stands in a courtyard of the former Ministry of Finance.

Other collections illustrate the civilizations that flourished to the east of Mesopotamia, on the plateau to which the invading Iranians gave their name at the end of the 2nd millenium, and at the foot of this plateau. They are painted ceramics, animal-shaped vases, figures of votaries from ancient Susiana, from the sixth to the middle of the 4th millennium. Elamite works such as the *Smiling God*, which was formerly covered in gold plate, and the massive bronze statue of *Queen Napirasu*, show the Mesopotamian influence on the kingdom of Susa during the third and second millennia; others, like the huge **Capital adorned with half-length bulls 13**, that topped one of the columns of the palace of Darius (521-485 BC) at Susa, testify to the grandeur of the Achaemenid kingdom of Persia. From the same building comes the glazed brick panel representing **Archers of the Guard 14**, the "Immortals", the elite of the magnificent army that was defeated by the Greeks at Marathon. Parthian terracotta pieces (200 BC-300 AD) are derived from Hellenic art, and luxury items from the Sassani period (224-651) include a **Royal bust 15** from the late 6th century AD which, in contrast, reflects the vigorous revival of Iranianism on the eve of the Arab conquest.

10 Code of Hammurabi, king of Babylon
1792-1750 BC
Richelieu 3, Ground Floor

11 Sargon II of Assyria and one of his ministers
End of 8th century BC
Richelieu 3, Ground Floor

12 Assyrian winged bull

Khorsabad, 8th century BC

Richelieu 3, Ground Floor

Numerous bronze objects from the civilizations in this area attest to the originality of the art of the high valleys of Luristan, on the eastern edge of the Iranian plateau, in the Iron Age, including weapons, standards, votive pins and hatchets, and **plaques from horses' bits 16**, decorated with genii, animals and stylized monsters.

This collection ends with antiquities from the evant. From Palestine, the Holy Land of the Bible, come numerous objects found in the Negev desert, some of which date back to the 4th millenium.

Several monuments from the Syro-Phoenician region go back to the Roman period, such as the Mithreum of Sidon and the fine ensemble of Palmyrian sculptures; others are contemporary with the Persian domination, like the sarcophagi from Sidon (5th to 4th centuries BC), which bear the unmistakable mark of the dual influence of Egypt and Ionia; still others belong to high antiquity, such as the supremely precious pieces discovered at Byblos and, especially, at Ras-Shamra, the ancient Ugarit, the point at which the Syrian, Egyptian and Mycenean cultures met during the 2nd millennium 17.

The no less complex history of Cyprus, from the Neolithic Age (circa 4000 BC) until the Roman era, is abundantly illustrated by a series of vases, terracotta figurines 18, jewelry and sculptures, while the Punic and Libyco-Punic monuments brought from Tunisia and Algeria evoke the distant past of the Phoenician civilization.

The Islamic Art Section attached to the Oriental Antiquities department displays its collections in the twelve new rooms on the mezzanine of the Richelieu Wing. The varied architecture of the exhibition space has facilitated a chronological museum circuit leading from the

13 Capital from the Apadana

Susa, late 6th century BC

Sully 4, Ground Floor

14 Archers of the Guard of Darius I

Susa, 521-485 BC

Sully 4, Ground Floor

15 Sassanid royal bust

6th century AD

Sully 4, Ground Floor

early Islamic period down through the great modern Safavid, Ottoman and Mogul Empires, complemented in the middle and at the end of the visit by thematic displays.

Outstanding in both their artistic quality and technique, the objects come from different countries between Spain and India, and include the **Ivory pyxis** [19] dated 968 and marked with the name Al Mughira, the Umayyad Prince of Spain, the 13th century Iranian ceramic **Cup with a huntsman on horseback** [20], the famous silver and gold-inlaid copper bowl from Syria or Egypt (circa 1300), known as the **Saint Louis baptistery** [21], the Ottoman ceramic **Peacock plate** [22] from the 16th century workshops of Iznick and the expressive jade *Horse head* inlaid with gold and rubies which formed the hilt of a weapon from Mogul India.

An interesting aspect of this section is the presentation of large groups of objects, ceramics, metalwork or glassware, which give an insight into the artistic production of a certain period of a specific technique. This particularly concerns ceramics from the Abbasid, Seljuk and Ottoman periods, Ayyubid, Mamluk and Farsistan metalwork, as well as Syro-Egyptian enamelled glassware. The group of Egyptian woodwork and pieces from the Susa digs should also be noticed.

16 **Plaque from a Luristan bridle-bit**
8th century BC

Sully 4, Ground Floor

17 Gold cup, with wild buffalo hunt
Ras-Shamra, 14th century BC

Sully 4, Ground Floor

18 Mother and Child
Cypriot idol, circa 2000 BC

Sully 4, Ground Floor

31

19 Al Mughira pyxis

Cordoba, 968 AD

Richelieu 3, Mezzanine

20 Cup with a huntsman on horseback

Iran, 13th century AD

Richelieu 3, Mezzanine

21 Bowl *known as the* Baptistery of Saint Louis
Syria or Egypt, circa 1300 AD
Richelieu 3, Mezzanine

22 Peacock plate
Iznik, 16th century AD
Richelieu 3, Mezzanine

33

Egyptian Antiquities

Another department that is world-famous in the field of archeology but of earlier creation (1816) than the preceding one is the Department of Egyptian Antiquities. It has been steadily enriched by donations and purchases, while a number of French scholars, beginning with its founder and first curator, Jean-François Champollion, the decipherer of the hieroglyphics, have contributed their discoveries. Today, its collections make it possible to trace the civilization and art of ancient Egypt throughout the entire continuity of their development, from their origins down to the Christian era. They are exhibited on the ground floor of the southeast quarter of the Square Courtyard buildings, on the so-called Egyptian staircase and on the first floor of the south wing, in a series of rooms overlooking the courtyard. These rooms are known as the Charles X Museum because of the decorations executed in 1827-1833, which confer considerable historical interest upon them. Reorganization of museum space will enable the department to extend its collections to the ground floor and first floor of the east wing on the Square Courtyard. During this period of renovation, there will be temporary displays of selected major works at various points throughout the museum.

For many observers, the most attractive feature of this department is its exceptionally rich documentation on the life and customs of the ancient Nile Valley inhabitants. These are illustrated by innumerable texts, pictorial representations and all manner of everyday objects (weapons, tools, recipients, furniture, clothing, toilet articles, jewelry, games, toys, scribes' accessories, musical instruments, etc.) **23**, **31**, **35**, **36**. The majority of the visitors, however, are chiefly interested in the brilliant array of masterpieces, some of which rank among the most famous in Egyptian art. The first manifestation of this art is illustrated by the **Guebel-el-Arak knife 24**

23 Trigonal harp
Saïte period, 7th-6th centuries BC

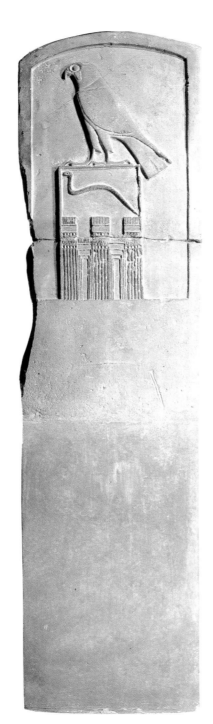

24 Guebel-el-Arak knife

Predynastic period, circa 3300-3200 BC

25 Serpent-king stele

Thinite period, circa 3100 BC

26 Head of King Djedefre

Old Kingdom, circa 2570 BC

35

(circa 3300-3200 BC) whose ivory handle is adorned with war and hunting scenes. The Asian influence, predominant in the predynastic era, clearly emerges here. It was during the Thinite period, under the first two dynasties, that Egyptian sculpture acquired its own original style, achieving a high technical level as early as the first centuries of the 3rd millennium. One striking example is a limestone monument dating from around 3100 BC, from the royal necropolis at Abydos, the **Stele of King Wadji 25** the so-called Serpent King. Its restrained, majestic decoration represents the facade to the king's palace, joining a vertical projection of its surrounding walls. Inside them is sculptured a snake, the hieroglyphic sign for this king's name. The whole is topped by the image of a falcon, the sacred animal of the god Horus, incarnation and protector of the Egyptian dynasty.

The creations of this archaic era, the works of ancient Egypt (2700-2200 BC) - carved of stone or wood, statues or bas-reliefs-are outstanding for their grandeur. Under the 4th and 5th dynasties, this grandeur was enhanced by a vigorous realism, which gives a look of unmistakable veracity to the specimens in the Louvre. This is especially evident in the dark pink quartzite head of King **Djedefre 26**, which was probably part of a sphinx, or, despite their mutilated state, in the deeply moving wooden statues of a **Memphite official and his wife 27**. This concern with intensely expressing the personality of the individual portrayed is brought to a climax in one of the best known works of ancient Egypt, the **Squatting Scribe 28**. This painted figure was discovered in a chapel at Saqquara, and possibly represents Kaï, a provincial administrator of whom the department possesses another statue found in the same tomb. Anonymous or not, this personage, rush-pen in hand and papyrus spread over his lap, fascinates

27 Memphite official and his wife
Old Kingdom, circa 2350-2200 BC

28 Squatting Scribe
Old Kingdom, circa 2500 BC

29 Amenemhatankh,
"chief of the prophets"
Middle Kingdom, circa 1850 BC

37

the beholder with his expressive physiognomy, his eyes glittering with intelligence, gazing attentively at whoever is dictating to him. The impression is enhanced by the eyes inlaid with opaque white quartz for the cornea, rock crystal for the iris and ebony for the pupil. The Middle Kingdom (2060-1786 BC) under the 11th and 12th dynasties continued to aim at realism, but already a trend toward idealization had set in. This is demonstrated by two items in the Louvre collection : the starkly designed yet harmonious sandstone statue of **Amenemhatankh**, "**Chief of the Prophets**" **29**, and the stuccoed, painted wooden figure of the graceful, slender **Offering Bearer 30**, delicately modelled under her transparent tunic overlaid with pearl netting.

The trend toward increasingly subtle idealization asserted itself under the New Kingdom (circa 1555-1080 BC), an incomparably glorious and prosperous period in the history of the Nile Valley. The absolute power of the pharaohs, the glittering life at court and the wealth of the ruling class gave rise to a truly "classic" art which best expressed the Egyptian people's ideal of beauty. In this aesthetic, grandeur and nobleness are tempered by grace and gentleness. It is not easy to choose among all the masterpieces in the department that testify to this evolution. Many visitors are attracted by the diorite statue of **Nephthys 32**, inscribed with the name of Amenophis III (circa 1403-1365 BC). The goddess's figure is represented with sober elegance, in a standing position, pressing a papyriform sceptre against her body. Others focus on a painted limestone relief from the tomb of **Seti I 33** (circa 1303-1290 BC), in the Valley of the Kings. It depicts the goddess Hathor in a splendid tunic, holding out to the sovereign her emblematic necklace. This is one of the finest examples showing the sensitivity and charm of the art of the New Kingdom.

30 Offering bearer
Middle Kingdom, circa 2000-1800 BC

31 Stele of Antef
High official Thutmosis III, circa 1490-1439 BC

32 The goddes Nephthys
New Kingdom, circa 1400 BC

A work situated chronologically between the two noted above emerges as all the more surprising, i.e. the extraordinary sandstone bust of **Amenophis IV-Akhenaton 34** (circa 1365-1349 BC), presented by Egypt to France in gratitude for the latter's role in saving the Nubian monuments. This huge head is representative of a brief revolution, expressed in art as well as in religion by a peculiar naturalism: it is carved so as to be seen from below – its summit is four meters above the ground – and it is typical of the official statuary of the early Amarnian period.

Here is an art animated by a deeply introspective realism, which is not afraid to exaggerate or even to commit excesses in order to reveal the intense spiritual life of the "seer" of Aton.

Other works of fine quality illustrate the efforts of Egyptian sculptors under the last native dynasties to revive the realism typical of Old Kingdom art. An elegant wooden statuette from the 30th dynasty (380-342 BC) is especially characteristic of this archaistic tendency, associated with a stylized elongation of the body. It represents a man standing, garbed in a long tunic, whose shaven head shows that he exercised some priestly function **37**.

The last days of Ancient Egypt, the Ptolemaic, Roman and Byzantine periods are also represented in the Louvre by a wide array of antiquities. Coptic art is so lavishly represented that an entire section has been devoted to it. Architectural fragments, reliefs of stone and wood, tapestries and garments, liturgical bronzes, ivories, glassware and ceramics reveal successively the pharaonic and above all Greco-Roman sources of this art, from its beginnings in the 4th century AD, its zenith during the Christian era (from the 5th to the 7th century) and, finally, after the Arab

33 The goddes Hathor protecting Seti I
New Kingdom, circa 1300 BC

34 Amenophis IV-Akhenaton
Circa 1365-1349 BC

35 Swimming girl and duck cosmetic spoon
14th century BC

conquest (641), its prolongation down to the 12th century. The rearrangement of the Coptic collections has also made it possible to partially reconstruct, from elements of its internal and external architecture and decoration, a church that was built in the 6th century and used until at least the ninth century: that of the Saint Apollo monastery at Baouït, a village in Middle Egypt. An extremely beautiful painting on wood from the monastery chapel, depicting **Christ protecting the Abbot Mena 38** (the head of the convent, 7th century AD), has been placed near the posts of the triumphal arch.

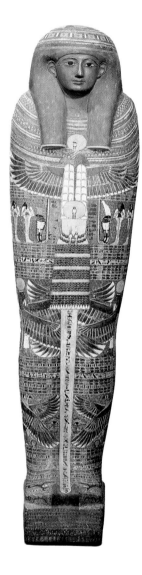

36 Sarcophagus of Chancellor Imenimet
(back, front and lid interior)
8th century BC

37 Anonymous priest
Late Period, 4th century BC
Wood

38 Christ protecting Abbot Mena
7th century AD

43

Greek, Etruscan and Roman Antiquities

The third archeological department traces its origins back to a Museum of Antiquities that was opened in the Louvre in 1800. To the royal collections in this initial foundation were added numerous works brought back from Italy after the French military victories, although only a small number remained after the restitutions effected by the allies in 1815. However, additional Greek, Etruscan and Roman antiquities soon began arriving to enrich the museum, and a steady stream of acquisitions, down to modern times, have made this department one of the main world centers of classical archeology. Its collections fill the Daru gallery, the Sphinx courtyard and the ground floor of the southwest quarter of the buildings around the Square Courtyard, as well as the rooms on the first floor of the south wing of this courtyard, overlooking the Seine, and the Henri II Room and the Bronze Room in the west wing. The new facilities envisaged by the Greater Louvre project confirm the Department of Greek, Etruscan and Roman Antiquities in the rooms and galleries it already occupies, while adding to it those areas beneath the Daru gallery which look northward across the Visconti courtyard, along with half of the first floor gallery contained by the Square Courtyard's south wing. Structural alterations for this purpose are now under way.

There is no chapter in the history of the art of antiquity, from the origins of Hellenism 39 to the last days of the Roman empire, that is not illustrated here either simultaneously or successively, and often with great distinction, by

marbles, bronzes, ceramics, gold and silver work, ivories, glasswork and frescoes.

This brilliant review is illustrated by such a large number of masterpieces of sculpture that selection is difficult. For the archaic period extending from the 7th century BC to the beginning of the 5th century AD, two items are worthy of note, i.e. the Doric **Auxerre Goddess 40** and the Ionian **Kore of Samos 41**. A comparison clearly shows the difference between the two principal currents underlying Greek art. The first piece – whose name stems from the fact that it was part of a collection from the vicinity of Auxerre – is one of the earliest known examples of Greek sculpture (circa 630 BC). The small, firmly built body stands with its feet joined, sheathed in a stiff tunic, bound at the waist by a wide belt, the shoulders covered by a short cape. A heavy, Egyptian-style wig covers the head. The uncluttered starkness of the style shows that it initiated in Crete. The second piece is more recent (circa 560 BC), and the cylindrical form, attesting to a Mesopotamian influence, indicates a very different approach: the delicate modelling of barely-suggested forms, the mysterious life that seems to animate them, the lightness and elegance of the draperies are characteristic of Ionia, whence it comes. A pendant to this ancient figure of Kore, which exactly resembles it, was recently discovered in the same sanctuary at Samos. The two statues, which probably stood on a plinth brought to light by the excavation, carry identical dedications to the goddess Hera, by a certain Cheramyes. Among the other pieces in the Louvre that bear witness to Greek archaism,

39 Cycladic idol

Keros, second half of 3rd millenium

Marble

40 Auxerre Goddess

Circa 630 BC

Denon 8, Ground Floor

41 Kore of Samos

Circa 560 BC

Denon 8, Ground Floor

45

mention should also be made of the **Rampin head 42** (circa 550 BC), a "masterpiece of intense delicacy and decorative charm" (J. Charbonneaux). It was part of the statue of a victorious horseman (originally in a group of two) whose torso and part of the body of whose horse are in the Acropolis Museum in Athens, along with other fragments of the ensemble.

The classical period, especially the 5th century, is represented in the Louvre collections by various pieces of high quality three-dimensional sculpture, such as the famous *Laborde Head*, which mingles gentleness, purity and energy. This head has been identified as that of the Nike driving Athena's chariot which decorated the west pediment of the Parthenon in Athens. Here again, it is through the juxtaposition of two essential works-reliefs, as it happens, that we can best understand the definitive progress accomplished by Greek art in the course of one century and the artistic characteristics of each of the two main schools from which it grew. These are a **Metope 43**, from the temple of Zeus at Olympia, built between 470 and 460 BC, and a fragment of the **Panathenaic procession 44** from the Parthenon, executed, like the Laborde head, between 442 and 432 BC. The strong, simple composition in intersecting diagonals of *Hercules Fighting the Cretan Bull*, the firm, robust forms of the bodies, and the somewhat stark modelling that makes the muscles seem to stand out by accentuating the shadows, are typical of the Doric technique. The *Ergastine*-sprung, like the entire decoration of the Parthenon, from Phidias's imagination-are no less characteristic of the Attic art which, in a new and harmonious way, combines the contrasting qualities of Doric and Ionic. This solemn procession of maidens who have woven the veil to be offered every four years to Athena reveals extreme care in its execution, discreet skill in its

42 Rampin head
Mid-6th century BC
Denon 8, Ground Floor

43 Hercules and the Cretan bull

Olympia, circa 460 BC

44 The Ergastines, frieze of the Panathenaics

Parthenon, 442-432 BC

Sully 7, Ground Floor

47

rhythm and a majesty both lively and graceful in its attitudes, which impart a feeling of true perfection.

From the 4th century on, Greek artists were increasingly attracted by truthfulness to human realities, and gradually abandoned the classical ideal. Scopas's pathos, Praxiletes's sensuality, Lysippus's heroic style paved the way for Hellenistic sculpture. Numerous works on exhibit in the Louvre testify to this evolution. Among the masculine types alone, there is the **Apollo Sauroctonus 45**, the original of which was created by Praxiteles in about 350 BC, and the **Borghese Gladiator 46**, by an artist of the first century BC, Agasias of Ephesus, clearly inspired by Lysippus.

Two statues of this period deserve mention because of their contribution to the world fame of the Louvre Museum, i.e. the **Winged Victory of Samothrace 47** and the **Venus of Milo 48**. The former, poised upright with spread wings at a galley prow, seems to be resisting the wind, which is flattening the soft folds of fabric against the body. It presumably commemorated a Rhodian naval victory at the end of the third or beginning of the 2nd century BC. At Samothrace, the 'Winged Victory' stood in a great niche towering above an "architectural landscape". Since the 1950 discovery of this statue's open right hand, it is assumed that the figure's right arm was stretched high to announce the victory. The statue of Aphrodite, an original discovered in 1820 on the island of Milo, is considered as a masterpiece of antique art and, in general, as one of the most perfect examples of female beauty. Despite the serene facial expression, which was originally thought to suggest the genius of Praxiteles, the stylistic features of this statue offer serious grounds for dating it from the late 2nd century BC. These features are "the proportions of the body, the fluidity of the lines, the deliberate

45 Apollo Sauroctonus
Replica of the Praxiteles, circa 350 BC
Sully 7, Ground Floor

46 Borghese Gladiator
Ist century BC
Sully 7, Ground Floor

47 The Victory of Samothrace
Late 3rd-early 2nd century BC
Denon 8, 1st Floor

contrast between the elaborate folds of the draperies and the nudity of the torso" (J. Charbonneaux).

A considerable amount of space in the Louvre's collections is devoted to sculptures of the Roman period. All of them demonstrate to varying degrees the artistic debt owed to Greece and the Hellenic world by Rome and its provinces. However, the numerous portraits and historical reliefs represent two branches in which there was real originality at that period. The abundant series of statues, busts and head-effigies of emperors, members of the imperial family or private citizens-constitute a veritable history of portraiture, from the time of the Republic down to the Late Empire. Some of these pieces rank among the masterpieces of the genre. They include the **Bust of Agrippa** 49 , Augustus's associate and son-in-law; the basalt head of *Livia*, Augustus's wife, and the exquisitely moving head of a **Young Prince of the Antonine family** 50 . Similarly, it is possible to retrace, from the late 2nd century BC to the second century AD, the evolution of the historical reliefs that constituted the main adornment of Roman commemorative buildings. The oldest, and unquestionably the most typical, of these "carved pictures" in the Louvre is the frieze that adorned one side of a large, rectangular base consecrated to the temple of Neptune in Rome, to which-presumably by mistake-was given the title of **Altar of Domitius Ahenobarbus** 51 (the other three sides of this frieze are in the Munich Museum of Sculpture). It mainly depicts the sacrifice of the Suovetaurilia; on either side of the altar, in the central part, are the god Mars and a magistrate, probably in the act of consecrating it. Beside this, a fragment of the frieze of the famous **Ara Pacis** 52 , the altar of peace consecrated in Rome by Augustus in 9 BC, appears more Grecian because of the quality of the line, the variety of

48 **Venus of Milo**

Late 2nd century BC

Sully 7, Ground Floor

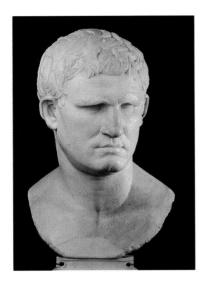

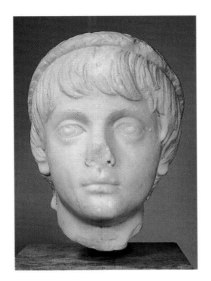

49 Bust of Agrippa

Early 1st century AD

Denon 8, Ground Floor

50 Portrait of a Young Prince of the Antonine Family

160 AD

Denon 8, Ground Floor

51 Altar of Domitius Ahenobarbus

(central part)

End 2nd-beginning 1st century BC

Denon 8, Ground Floor

51

attitudes and draperies and the type of relief. The procession is nonetheless Roman, with its varied perspectives, densely clustered figures and distinctive realism; this scene is not idealized as it is in the procession of the Ergastines. The bronzes, also, are fully as important for an understanding of this sculpture-especially in the case of a masterpiece like the **Apollo of Piombino 53**, the date of which is less certain than its undisputed quality: opinions on this score vary from 500 BC to the first century AD. They help us to comprehend various aspects of the Greek, Etruscan and Roman civilizations. In the room devoted to them, statues, statuettes and small figures are displayed side by side with great numbers of other objects, interesting either because of their ornamentation, or for the purposes for which they were designed, or for both; they include **mirrors 54**, cists, lamps, armour, furniture and sundry utensils. Although Greco-Roman gold and silver work was less abundant, it is represented in the Louvre by a magnificent collection of gold jewelry and numerous silver pieces; the most famous of these were discovered at *Boscoreale*, near Pompei **55**.

Several fine examples of frescoes and, indirectly, of **mosaics 56**, testify to the quality of Greco-Roman painting, but in this realm of antique art the museum is primarily known for its vase collections. The world-famous collection of Greek vases, exhibited in the Campana Gallery-named after a very large collection purchased in 1863-provides a complete panorama of all the schools and styles, ranging from the so-called geometric ceramics (9th-8th centuries BC) to the most recent Hellenistic productions (2nd century BC) **57, 58, 59**.
These are historical documents, and also original works of art (whereas the great majority of Greek sculptures and paintings are known only through copies dating from the Roman period). Few

52 Frieze of the Ara Pacis
(fragment)
Late 1st century BC
Denon 8, Ground Floor

53 Apollon of Piombino

Circa 500 BC

Denon 8, Ground Floor

54 Engraved Etruscan mirror

3rd century BC

Denon 8, Ground Floor

bear the signatures of the great masters, such as Exekias (circa 550-530 BC) -Attic red-figured vases- and Euphronios (520-500 BC) -Attic red-figured vases. The last room of this gallery houses the finest pieces of a major collection of small terracotta figures, especially known for the items crafted in the workshops of Tanagra **60** and Myrina during the Hellenistic period.

55 **Goblet from Boscoreale**
1st century AD
Sully 7, 1st Floor

56 The Judgment of Paris,
Mosaic from Antioch 2nd century AD
Denon 8, Ground Floor

57 Proto-Corinthian vase in the form of an owl

7th century BC

58 Bell-idol

Boeotia, circa 700 BC

⁵⁹ Heracles and Antaeus
Wine chalice, signed by Euphronios, circa 510 BC

⁶⁰ The "Sophoclean Woman"
Tanagra, end 4th century BC

57

Paintings

Although the Louvre's collection of paintings may not be the largest of any museum in the world, it is unquestionably the most complete. It originated with the "Cabinet of Pictures" constituted at Fontainebleau by François I. This collection was greatly enriched by Louis XIV-an inventory taken in 1709-1710 lists nearly fifteen hundred paintings-and, after the fall of the monarchy, it was further increased by property confiscated from the church and the émigrés, as well as by plunder from various European countries subsequent to the Revolutionary and Imperial conquests. It was considerably reduced by the restitutions made in 1815, but eventually got back into full stride, especially from the Second Empire on. Since that time there have been many donations and purchases, with the department following a policy of eclectic acquisitions in accordance with the diversity of its existing bequests. The collection occupies the entire second floors of the Richelieu Wing and of the

Anonymous
61 Portrait of King John the Good
Circa 1360

Richelieu 3, 2nd Floor

Jean FOUQUET
62 Portrait of King Charles VII
Circa 1445

Richelieu 3, 2nd Floor

Enguerrand QUARTON
63 Pietà of Villeneuve-lès-Avignon
Circa 1460

Richelieu 3, 2nd Floor

Square Courtyard, as well as the part of the palace situated on the first floor of the Denon Wing to the west of the Apollo Gallery, specifically including the Square Room, the Great Gallery and the Estates Room.

It is not surprising that two-thirds of the paintings in the Louvre should belong to the French school. To begin with the most outstanding items, there is, first of all, the **Pietà of Villeneuve-lès-Avignon 63**, an austere and grandiose masterpiece from the late Middle Ages, now attributed to Enguerrand Quarton, who hailed from the Laon diocese but is known to have worked in Provence from 1444 to 1446. There is also the anonymous **Portrait of King Jean the Good 61**, painted in about 1360. This is the oldest known French easel painting, as well as the first of a type for which Jean Fouquet, notably, became known during the next century, particularly through his **Charles VII 62**, in which the compact arrangement carries overtones of the Gothic style. This style of painting, in which Clouet excelled, was still flourishing in the 16th century, when the Italian decorators whom François I had brought to Fontainebleau introduced into France a mannerist art fraught with elegance and subtlety, as evidenced in **Diana the Huntress 64**, by an unknown master (circa 1550), which is thought to be an idealized portrait of King Henri II's favourite, Diane de Poitiers. Few of the painters influenced by the Fontainebleau school had such a powerful personality as Antoine Caron. His **Massacre of the Triumvirs 65**, dated 1566, is strongly allegorical, after the fashion of the day, and constitutes a barely veiled allusion to the initial horrors of the Wars of Religion.

At the outset of the 17th century, following an initial period of crisis, French artists endeavoured to revive their art directly in Italy, particularly in Rome.

Fontainebleau school
64 Diana the Huntress
Circa 1550
Richelieu 3, 2nd Floor

Antoine CARON
65 Massacre of the Triumvirs
1566
Richelieu 3, 2nd Floor

Most of them, like Valentin and Vignon, found what they were seeking in the works of Caravaggio, with his religious themes and scenes of everyday life, and his dramatic, strongly contrasted lighting [99]. Georges de La Tour was also influenced by this powerful master of European painting. He had a predilection for homely night-time interiors imbued with an atmosphere of mystery produced by the flickering light of a torch or candle, and also for a very personal simplification of forms and soberly harmonious colors, which are equally original [66, 67]. The three Le Nain brothers were even more attracted by the realities of everyday life; of the two, it was definitely Louis who, gifted with a sensitivity devoid of sentimentality, best expressed both the rusticity and the dignity of the lives of humble folk [68].

Nicolas Poussin, master par excellence of French classicism, theorist, philosopher and poet, spent nearly his entire life in Rome. More so than any other artist of his time, he was obsessed by a desire for perfection in his art, in which the landscapes that were the settings for his biblical, mythological and historical subjects eventually became his main, theme [69]. Claude Gellée- known as Le Lorrain-was also a "Roman" and a landscape painter, although less intellectual and more anecdotal and lyrical than Poussin. He was primarily concerned with the study of light, with its variations at different times of the day and its reflections in water [70], and he is sometimes considered as one of the precursors of Impressionism.

Portrait-painting was not neglected by French 17th-century artists, and it gave a number of rich temperaments the chance to fully express themselves. Philippe de Champaigne, of Flemish origin, was the official painter to Louis XIII and Richelieu, and eventually became the recognized iconographer of

Georges de LA TOUR
66 **Saint Thomas**
Circa 1630

Sully 4, 2nd Floor

Georges de La Tour

67 Saint Joseph in the Carpenter's Shop

Circa 1640

Sully 4, 2nd Floor

Jansenism: his greatest masterpiece, entitled **Ex-voto, 1662** **71**, executed in gratitude to God for the recovery of his daughter Catherine, a nun at Port-Royal, depicts her beside Mother Agnès Arnauld at the moment at which the miracle was revealed to the abbess. This austere, fervent act of thanksgiving has little in common with the sprightly, academic manner of Charles Le Brun's *Chancellor Séguier* (circa 1655-1657) or with Hyacinthe Rigaud's solemn, sumptuous **Louis xiv** **72** (1701), but both these compositions are also admirable for their subtle psychological observation of faces.

At the dawn of the 18th century, Antoine Watteau's subjects and techniques opened up new possibilities for painting. He frequently drew his inspiration from scenes and characters in contemporary French and Italian theatre plays, and his portrait of an actor, entitled **Gilles** **73**, is at once symbolic and personal-it is considered by some to be a self-portrait. This delicate colorist and no less remarkable draftsman gave his genius full play by transposing these subjects into the make-believe world of dreams and pageantry. As the painter of *fêtes galantes*, he was admitted to membership in the Royal Academy of Painting and Sculpture on August 28th, 1717, on which occasion he exhibited *The Pilgrimage to Cythera*, a second version of which is now in the Charlotenburg Palace in Berlin. Watteau's sensitive, poetic art set the tone for several decades of French painting. It is found in the elegant genre of François Boucher, although his art was more licentious and decorative; in that of Honoré Fragonard **74**, more intimist and executed with greater brio; and in the still-lifes and portraits**121** of Jean-Baptiste Chardin, which are linked with the trend toward realism. Even the moralistic Jean-Baptiste Greuze made a concession to the vogue for gracility when he painted **The Broken Pitcher** **75** (1777).

LOUIS LE NAIN
68 **Peasant Family**
Circa 1643

Sully 4, 2nd Floor

Nicolas Poussin
69 Shepherds in Arcadia
Circa 1640
Richelieu 3, 2nd Floor

During the second half of the 18th century, an increasingly strong reaction set in against a style of painting that had begun to seem unduly witty, too charming, overly concerned with everyday realities. Archeological discoveries revived admiration for Greco-Roman antiquity, while at the same time there emerged a generalized idealism that demanded a simpler, more serious and more heroic type of art. This aspiration spawned the neoclassical movement, of which **The Oath of the Horatians 76**, the big success at the 1785 Salon, was a kind of manifesto. The work of Louis David contains all the elements of neoclassicism, i.e. the moral of historical grandeur of the subject, a composition with the rhythmic balance of an antique bas-relief, noble poses, anatomical precision and primary importance assigned to drawing rather than to color. The Revolution and, later, the Napoleonic epic afforded this imperious doctrinaire and his pupils a chance to give brilliant expression to their ideas. David was able to display all his talent for portrait-painting in **The Coronation 77**, done between 1805 and 1807, and **Bonaparte Visiting Victims of the Plague at Jaffa 78** was executed within the span of a few months by Antoine Gros: these are two of the Louvre's largest and most renowned canvases. In spite of this official blessing, however, neoclassicism did not reign unchallenged. The sensitivity and poetic charm of Pierre-Paul Prud'hon **79** prolonged the graceful manner of the 18th century, while foreshadowings of Romanticism were already evident in the work of Anne-Louis Girodet. Indeed, something of this same anticipation may perhaps be detected in the color and epic inspiration of the *Victims of the Plague at Jaffa*.

The Raft of the Medusa 80, presented at the 1819 Salon by Théodore Gericault, is often considered to be the first manifestation of French Romanticism in

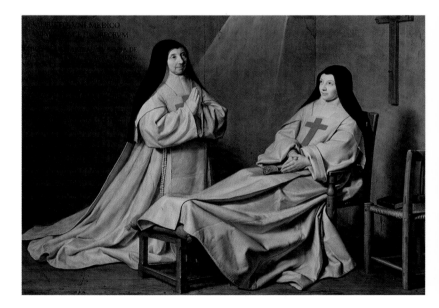

Claude Gellée, *known as* Le Lorrain
70 Seaport
1639
Richelieu 3, 2nd Floor

Philippe de Champaigne
71 Ex-voto, 1662
Sully 5, 2nd Floor

Hyacinthe RIGAUD
72 **Louis XIV in Coronation Robes**
1701
Sully 5, 2nd Floor

painting. This illustration of a contemporary human interest story (the survival of fifteen people shipwrecked after the sinking of a frigate that had set sail for Senegal in July 1816) is executed with a passion and dramatic force that rank it among the great masterpieces of French painting and that, in any case, justify its being displayed in the same gallery as the works of Eugène Delacroix, whose advent marked the triumph of the new school. Triumph of color, of movement, of emotion... This was a revolution, and one may justifiably wonder which of this brilliant painter's sixty-odd canvases best represent it. Many observers would cast their vote for **Lyberty Guiding de People 81**, inspired by the events of July 1830, though some prefer the more sober Delacroix of *The Taking of Constantinople by the Crusaders* (1841), in which the tumultuous movement of the preceding work is moderated and harmonized by the nobility of the composition. We should also be neglecting an essential aspect of this sumptuous colorist if we failed to mention the *Women of Algiers in their Apartment* (1834), in which light plays such an important part; nor could we understand his tormented nature if we forgot the **Portrait of Frederick Chopin 82**, (1838), which exposes all the anguish of romantic creation.

It is traditional to compare Delacroix with Jean-Dominique Ingres-the magician of colorful masses as against the poet of forms **122**, the admirer of the Venetians and of Rubens as against the admirer of the 15th century Florentines and of Raphael, devoted to the pure lines and arid subtle curves learned from the paintings on Greek vases; the ardent defender of the imagination as against the clear, realistic mind imbued with classical distinctness and honest observation.

Three paintings, each in its own way, typify the aesthetic of this serene, upright bourgeois who was nonetheless

Antoine WATTEAU

73 Gilles

Circa 1718

Sully 5, 2nd Floor

Honoré FRAGONARD
74 Women Bathing
Circa 1770
Sully 6, 2nd Floor

voluptuously inspired by the beauty of the female form. *The Apotheosis of Homer* (1827) is a composition designed to decorate a ceiling of the Louvre, where it was intended to constitute a profession of faith; the *Portrait of Monsieur Bertin* (1832), founder of the *Journal des Débats*, is an almost symbolic representation of the upper-middle class of the day; **The Turkish Bath** [84] (1862) is the synthesis and outcome of a lifetime's research devoted to the theme of women bathing. In time, an "Ingres School" also emerged; Theodore Chassériau successfully reconciled it with the art of his master's rival Delacroix, and his **Esther at her Toilet** [83] is worthy of both of them.

Romanticism revived an interest in nature, which played an important part in French painting from 1830 on. The Louvre possesses over one hundred and thirty canvases by Camille Corot, who illustrates this trend. Although he followed the classical tradition handed down by Poussin and Claude Lorrain, the poetic freshness of Corot's approach and an increasingly evident interest in the subtle play of light resulted in a freedom of plastic expression that reveals him as a forerunner of Impressionism [85, 86]. Most of the other landscape painters followed in the footsteps of the 17th-century Dutch painters; several of them settled on the edge of the Fontainebleau forest at Barbizon, which thereby gave its name to a school of painting. The most noteworthy of these, Theodore Rousseau [87], was soon followed there by Dupré, Diaz, Daubigny and Jacque. Altogether free of literary content, their landscapes exalted the beauty of nature, trees and water, with vibrant renderings of the general atmosphere, and of the variations in light at a given site at different times of the day. In so doing they anticipated the celebrated "series" of the Impressionists. Man is absent from most of the works of the Barbizon painters, a fact that has been seen as a denial of the

Jean-Baptiste GREUZE
75 The Broken Pitcher
1777
Sully 6, 2nd Floor

Louis DAVID
76 The Oath of the Horatians
1784
Denon 9, 1st Floor

Louis DAVID

77 **Coronation of Napoleon I at Notre-Dame de Paris, December 2nd 1804**

(detail)

1805-1807

Denon 9, 1st Floor

modern world, along with progress, industrialization and their accompanying social difficulties. In that regard they differed from Millet, Courbet and Daumier whose paintings glorified the lives of peasants and city-dwellers (these now hang in the Musée d'Orsay).

Antoine GROS
78 Bonaparte Visiting Victims of the Plague at Jaffa
1804

Denon 8, 1st Floor

Pierre-Paul PRUD'HON
79 The Empress Josephine
1805

Denon 9, 1st Floor

Théodore GÉRICAULT
80 **The Raft of the Medusa**
1819
Denon 8, 1st Floor

Eugène DELACROIX

81 Liberty Guiding the People

1830

Denon 8, 1st Floor

Eugène DELACROIX

82 Portrait of Frederick Chopin

1838

Sully 7, 2nd Floor

Théodore CHASSÉRIAU

83 **Esther at her Toilet**

1842

Sully 7, 2nd Floor

Jean-Dominique INGRES

84 **The Turkish Bath**

1862

Sully 7, 2nd Floor

Camille COROT

85 Souvenir de Mortefontaine

1864

Sully 7, 2nd Floor

Camille COROT

86 Lady in Blue

1874

Sully 7, 2nd Floor

Théodore ROUSSEAU

87 Road Leading out of the Forest of Fontainebleau

Sully 7, 2nd Floor

Of all the foreign schools, the Italian is best represented in the Louvre, partly because it provided the first, sumptuous royal collections of paintings, but also because it has always been highly appreciated in France. Every phase of its evolution, from the second half of the 13th century to the end of the 18th, is illustrated here by several world-famous masterpieces.

Two large panels, both from the church of San Francesco in Pisa, bear brilliant witness to the early days of Florentine art. One is Cimabue's majestic **Madonna of the Angels 88** (circa 1270), marking the onset of a reaction against the hieratism of Byzantine models in the freer, more human poses of the figures. The other is Giotto's *Saint Francis of Assisi receiving the Stigmata* (circa 1300), in which the artist achieved complete liberation. *The Bearing of the Cross*, executed by Simone Martini during his stay at the papal court in Avignon (1340-1344), is one wing panel of a small portable polyptych, the other elements of which are in the Musée Royal des Beaux-Arts in Antwerp and the Berlin-Dahlem museum. This painting, among those of the early masters of other Italian schools, exemplifies the significant contribution made by the artists of Siena.

During the *quattrocento* (15th century), under the dual influence of architecture and sculpture, Italian painting began to evolve in the direction of the Renaissance. Although Fra Angelico's **Coronation of the Virgin 90**, painted in 1434-1435 for the church of San Domenico in Fiesole, remains medieval in its choice of subject and mystic treatment, it points to a new orientation in the Louvre's collections. The scope and balance of its structure, the observance of perspective, the arrangement of the figures without regard for traditional organization-all these are clearcut signs of a modernism that becomes even more

CIMABUE
88 Madonna of the Angels
Circa 1270
Denon 10, 1st Floor

GIOTTO
89 Saint Francis Preaching to the Birds
Predella of the retable in the church of Saint Francis of Assisi, circa 1300
Denon 10, 1st Floor

Fra ANGELICO
90 The Coronation of the Virgin
1434-1435
Denon 10, 1st Floor

79

obvious in the scenes from the life of Saint Dominic shown in the predella. Paolo Uccello also emerged as an innovator when, in 1455, commissioned by the Medici family, he painted the episode from **The Battle of San Romano 91**, now in the possession of the Louvre: a second episode hangs in the Uffizi Galleries in Florence, while a third is in London's National Gallery. The care with which depth and volume are rendered by bold foreshortening, the decorative stylization of the forms, emphasized by bold coloring, give this work the monumental appearance of a high-relief. **The Calvary 92**, painted by Andrea Mantegna to decorate the central part of the predella of an altar-piece for the church of San Zeno, in Verona-its lateral parts are in the museum of Tours- is more finely wrought, more geometrical, more insightful. By Sandro Botticelli, who was torn between Christianism and humanism, there are two major compositions characterized by his sharp, sinuous brushstroke, his delicate, transparent colors, and his extremely refined style, ideally suited for expressing the mannered grace of mournful, mysterious allegories. These frescoes 93, datable 1483, come from the Villa Lemmi (near Florence), originally the property of the Tornabuoni family, friends of the Medicis.

The so-called Golden Age (late 15th to mid-16th century) of the Italian Renaissance is brilliantly illustrated in the Louvre. First and foremost, it boasts an array, unparalleled elsewhere in the world, of works by Leonardo da Vinci, beginning with the most universally admired and discussed of all paintings, the **Mona Lisa 94**. This portrait, which may reasonably be assumed to represent Mona Lisa Gherardini, who in 1495 was married to the Florentine patrician Francesco del Giocondo, is also known as *La Gioconda*. Leonardo da Vinci was so attached to this painting, done bet-

Paolo UCCELLO
91 The Battle of San Romano
Circa 1450-1455
Denon 10, 1st Floor

Sandro Botticelli

93 **Fresco from Villa Lemmi**

(detail)

Circa 1483

Denon 8, 1st Floor

Andrea Mantegna

92 **Calvary**

1459

Denon 10, 1st Floor

81

ween 1503 and 1506, that he brought it with him when François I invited him to France in 1516. He settled near Amboise, in the Château de Cloux, where he died three years later. The *Mona Lisa* thereupon became the most precious item in the king's "Cabinet of Paintings". Virtually everything has been said about the enigmatic smile, the marvelous modelling of the face, the shading off of the color values so that the light seems to glide over the forms, the misty, dreamlike atmosphere of the background landscape. In the same way, the mysterious poetry and the already perfect craftsmanship of the *Virgin of the Rocks*, commissioned in 1483 by the Brotherhood of the Conception of San Francesco Grande in Milan, have been the subject of continuous study. The same is true of the symbolism and spirituality of **The Virgin, the Child and Saint Anne 95** , a painting executed several years after the *Mona Lisa* and commissioned by the Servites of Florence for the high altar of their church.

Several of the paintings by Raphael that now hang in the Louvre once belonged to François I. This was presumably the case for **The Virgin and Child with Saint John the Baptist 96** , which, because of the rusticity of the scene, is traditionally known as *La Belle Jardinière*. All in all, it is the finest example in the museum's collections of the perfect harmony to which its artist aspired. A freer-style portrait painted by Raphael in 1514-1515 is hardly less well-known: it represents his friend *Balthazar Castiglione*, a poet and diplomat and "the finest knight in all the world", according to Emperor Charles V. Louis XIV acquired it from Mazarin's heirs in 1661. In the same year and from the same source, Correggio's *Antiope* (circa 1524-1525) was purchased for the royal collections. This work was well known in its day and its artistry is less intellectual, more relaxed in its sensuality.

Leonardo Da Vinci
94 **The Mona Lisa**
Circa 1503-1506
Denon 8, 1st Floor

Leonardo DA VINCI

95 **The Virgin, the Child and Saint Anne**

Circa 1506-1510

Denon 8, 1st Floor

This latter tendency eventually prevailed in Venice, where, until the end of the 16th century, the Venetian artists painted not for reasons of piety or to test their abilities, but simply to give direct expression to what they felt when viewing a landscape, draperies, or naked human flesh. In the place of the fineness of line and delicate modelling beloved of the Florentines, they preferred masses of light and color. This *maniera moderna* had Giorgione as its initiator and his pupil Titian as its most illustrious representative. Is the *Rustic Concert* the work of the master or of his disciple? It is dated 1510-1511 and was long attributed to Giorgione, but nowadays is viewed as being in all likelihood by Titian. Whatever the case, stylistic comparison reveals its close resemblance to the latter's **Entombment 97**, painted some fifteen years later and added to the royal collections, together with the *Rustic Concert*, in 1671. The Louvre possesses two outstanding examples of the decorative style splendidly developed by the Venetian painters of the following generations: Veronese's gigantic **Marriage at Cana 98**, which was commissioned in 1562 and completed in 1563 for the refectory of the San Giorgio Maggiore convent in Venice, and the sketch for the huge composition entitled *Paradise*, commissioned from Tintoretto in 1588 to adorn the Great Council Hall of the Serenissime in the palace of the Doges.

Toward the end of the 16th century a new kind of art began to develop in Italy. In 1585, in Bologna, the Carracci brothers founded an academy-the first school of fine arts-where they taught a more eclectic approach. This tended toward naturalism in Annibale Carracci's landscapes entitled *The Hunt* and *The Fishing Expedition*, in the Louvre. Caravaggio was more revolutionary, and his aesthetic and technique were to exert a strong influence over European painting, especially in France.

RAPHAEL
96 La Belle Jardinière
1507
Denon 8, 1st Floor

TITIAN
97 **The Entombment**
Circa 1525

Denon 9, 1st Floor

85

His **Death of the Virgin** **99**, commissioned
in 1605 for Rome's church of Santa
Maria in Trastevere, created a scandal
because of what was regarded as overly
plebeian realism accentuated by an
unduly dramatic contrast between the
zones of light and shadow. All this not-
withstanding, this painting compelled
admiration from those who recognized
it as foreshadowing a regeneration.

Eighteenth-century Venice witnessed the
last great days of Italian painting. Of
the works from this period in the
Louvre, the most noteworthy are those
of Francesco Guardi **100**, represented by
a series of ten canvases-out of the original twelve-commemorating the festivities
attendant upon the coronation of a doge,
Alvise Mocenigo IV.

VERONESE
98 **The Marriage at Cana**
(detail)
1563
Denon 9, 1st Floor

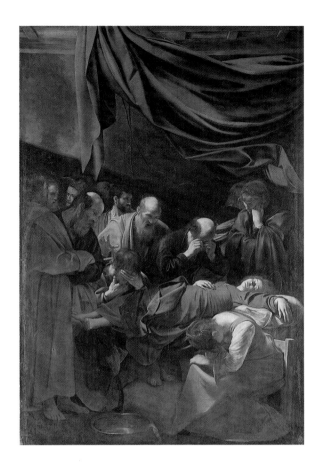

CARAVAGGIO
99 The Death of the Virgin
Circa 1605
Denon 9, 1st Floor

Francesco GUARDI
100 The Doge at Santa Maria della Salute
Circa 1770
Denon 10, 1st Floor

Although the Flemish and Dutch schools are less abundantly represented than the Italians in the Louvre, the museum does boast a large number of masterpieces from these two schools, now exhibited in the Richelieu Wing and of sufficient importance to provide an almost complete panorama.

From the earliest Flemish painters, the Louvre has two paintings of capital importance: Jan van Eyck's **Virgin of Autun** ₁₀₁ (circa 1435), which comes from the collegiate church of that city (to which it had been donated by Nicolas Rolin, chancellor of Burgundy); and Rogier van der Weyden's *Braque Triptych* (circa 1452), probably executed for Catherine of Brabant in memory of her late husband, Jehan Braque. Among the works of the latter half of the 15th century, several paintings by Hans Memling deserve mention, notably his **Portrait of an Old Woman** ₁₀₂ (circa 1470-1475). The 16th century works include **The Moneylender and his Wife** ₁₀₃ (1514), by Quentin Metsys-one of the pioneer examples of genre painting in the Netherlands-and Pieter Breughel the Elder's **Beggars** ₁₀₄ (1568), which has been interpreted as an allusion to the so-called "beggars' revolt" against the government of Philip II of Spain. Peter-Paul Rubens's supremacy in the Flemish school of the 17th century is brilliantly illustrated by the two admirable portraits of his second wife, Helena Fourment, and his children; by *The Village Fair* (circa 1635-1638), replete with teeming life, which was studied to advantage by several French artists (Watteau, Fragonard, Delacroix...); and, most importantly, by the huge decorative ensemble executed between 1622 and 1625 in honor of Queen Marie de' Medici, designed at her request to adorn a gallery in the Luxembourg palace. One of its best-known sections-another source of inspiration for the French artists noted above-is that entitled **Marie**

Jan VAN EYCK
101 The Virgin of Autun
Circa 1435
Richelieu 3, 2nd Floor

Hans MEMLING
102 Portrait of an Old Woman
Circa 1470-1475
Richelieu 3, 2nd Floor

Quentin METSYS
103 The Moneylender and his Wife
1514
Richelieu 3, 2nd Floor

de' Medici Landing at Marseille **105**. Of the
many portraits of Charles I of England
by Anton van Dyck, "painter in ordinary to the king", the one in the
Louvre **106** is considered to be the finest.
Similarly, the painting entitled *The Four
Evangelists* is regarded as one of the
most outstanding canvases from Jacob
Jordaens's early period.

Pieter BRUEGHEL the Elder
104 The Beggars
1568
Richelieu 3, 2nd Floor

Peter-Paulus RUBENS
105 Marie de' Medici landing at Marseilles
1622-1625
Richelieu 2, 2nd Floor

Anton Van Dyck

106 Portrait of Charles I of England

Circa 1635

Richelieu 2, 2nd Floor

In the Dutch collection, all the great names are excellently represented. They include Hieronymus Bosch, with his panel painting entitled **The Ship of Fools** 107, dating from the late 15th century, a semi-surrealist allegory stigmatizing the "follies" of taste and hearing and, more generally, the vices of the painter's time. Lucas van Leyden's fantastic landscape entitled *Lot and his Daughters* (circa 1509-1517) is a mannerist-style forerunner of the following century's Dutch "luminism". By Frans Hals there is a so-called "character portrait", **The Gypsy Girl** 108 (circa 1628), reminiscent of Caravaggio in its freedom and audacity. The subtle perfection of light, color and brushwork in Jan Vermeer of Delft is represented by **The Astronomer** 110 (1688- acquired by dation in 1983), and by the subtle perfection of light, color and brushwork in his **Lacemaker** 109 (1664) which admirably expresses the serenity of domestic life by bringing out its innate poetry. Elsewhere, Jacob van Ruisdael's *The Burst of Sunlight* is rightly classed among the world's greatest landscape paintings. The pride of this collection is the impressive array of Rembrandts: portraits, especially **self-portraits** 112, like the supremely moving one in which the artist depicts himself aged fifty-four, worn out by grief, hardship and solitude, yet still confident of his art; biblical scenes, including the famous *Pilgrims at Emmaus* (1648), in which the magical chiaroscuro and the utter simplicity of the composition combine to render the divine presence visible with an intensity seldom achieved by any artist; and **Bathsheba at her Toilet** 111 (1654), showing the subject holding the letter in which David declares his love. This is one of Rembrandt's rare nudes, for which his model was his devoted second wife, Hendrickje Stoffels.

Hieronymus BOSCH
107 The Ship of Fools
Circa 1490-1500
Richelieu 3, 2nd Floor

Frans HALS
108 The Gypsy Girl
1628-1630
Richelieu 2, 2nd Floor

Jan VERMEER of Delft
109 The Lacemaker

1664

Richelieu 2, 2nd Floor

Jan VERMEER of Delft
110 The Astronomer

1668

Richelieu 2, 2nd Floor

93

REMBRANDT

112 Portrait of the Painter in his Old Age

1660

Richelieu 2, 2nd Floor

The collection of German paintings is more modest, but it does feature several major items from the most glorious period of this school (late 15th century), including notably *The Descent from the Cross*, which formed the central part of a great triptych executed circa 1500 by the artist known as the Master of Saint Bartholomew (from the name of a retable in the Munich Museum); Albert Dürer's **Self-Portrait** 113 painted when the artist was aged twenty-two (1493), reportedly for his fiancée (he is holding a species of thistle, symbol of fidelity); a charming *Venus* (1529) by Lucas Cranach the Elder; Hans Holbein the Younger's most famous portrait, that of **Erasmus** 114, the "prince of humanism" (1523), writing his *Commentary on the Gospel of Saint Mark*.

Similarly, even though it has only a small place in the Louvre, the English school is brilliantly illustrated. For the 17th century, there are portraits by Sir Joshua Reynolds 115, founder of the Royal Academy; by his rival, Thomas Gainsborough; and by Sir Thomas Lawrence, painter to all the European courts. For the 19th century, there are the romantic landscapes of John Constable, Richard Parkes Bonington and Joseph M.W. Turner.

Albrecht Dürer
113 Self-Portrait

1493

Richelieu 3, 2nd Floor

Hans HOLBEIN the Younger
114 **Portrait of Erasmus**

1523

Richelieu 3, 2nd Floor

Sir Joshua REYNOLDS
115 **Master Hare**

1788-1789

Denon 10, 1st Floor

97

The Spanish collection is unquestionably less magnificent than the one that was Louis-Philippe's personal property; which, after being exhibited in the Louvre from 1838 to 1848, followed the king to his exile in London, where it was dispersed at auction in 1853. Today, it is still notable for a fine array of masterpieces: early-master paintings, such as Martorell's *Martyrdom of Saint-George* (circa 1430-1435); El Greco's **Christint on the Cross 116** (circa 1580), highly typical of this artist's manner; and fine examples of Spain's artistic Golden Age (17th century), such as Ribera's *Clubfooted Boy* (1642); Zurburán's **Funeral of St. Bonaventura 117** (about 1630; Murillo's *Beggar Boy* (1650); The portrait (attributed to Velazquez) of The Infanta Margarita, Philip IV's daughter (circa 1655); and Carreño de Miranda's *Mass for the founding of the Order of the Trinitarians* (1666). Last but not least, there are several portraits by Goya, including the splendid **Marquesa de la Solana 118** (circa 1791-1794) from the Beistegui Collection.

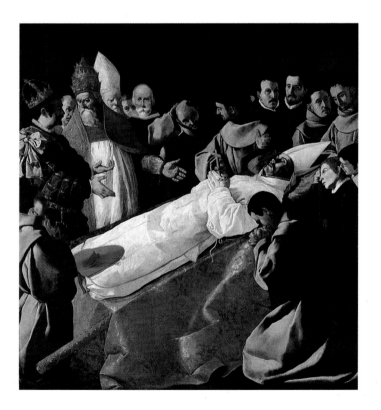

El Greco
116 Christ on the Cross
Circa 1580

Denon 10, 1st Floor

Zurbaran
117 The Funeral of Saint Bonaventura
Circa 1630

Denon 10, 1st Floor

GOYA

118 Portrait of the Marquesa de la Solana

Circa 1791-1794

Sully 4, 2nd Floor

Graphic Arts

Stored for protection against variations of light and temperature, the Louvre's reserve of drawings, along with its ensemble of engravings from the Edmond de Rothschild Collection, is located in the Flore Wing of the museum, but cannot be left on permanent display. This rich and varied collection may be viewed by amateurs on request to the curator's office. Temporary exhibitions on specific themes are regularly organized in a room adjoining the main collection, or near the Pyramid; these may be visited by the general public during ordinary museum opening hours. In addition, a selection of drawings by the Northern schools, of Le Brun's cartoons and 18th century French pastels and miniatures is exhibited on a rota system in the painting sections.

Leonardo Da Vinci
119 Isabelle d'Este
Circa 1490
Black chalk, red chalk and pastel

Rembrandt
120 The Canal at Amersfoort
Circa 1655
Pen-and-ink and brown wash drawing

Jean-Baptiste CHARDIN
121 **Self-Portrait with green eyeshade**
1775
Pastel

Jean-Dominique INGRES
122 **The Stamaty Family**
1818
Black lead pencil drawing

Sculptures

The sculpture department came into being when the Museum of French Monuments was discontinued in 1817, under the Restoration. Part of its collection was thereupon moved from the convent of the Minor Augustinians to the Louvre, and it has been continuously added to so that it now constitutes as complete a history as possible of French sculpture, from its origins to the end of the 19th century. The exhibits are arranged in chronological order in the ground floor rooms of the Richelieu Wing looking onto the two large Marly and Puget Courtyards.

First, there are the Romanesque sculptures, most of them executed strictly on the basis of the architectural fragments they adorn. One example is the representation of **Daniel in the Lions' Den 123**, from the late 11th century, on a recarved capital from the church of Sainte Geneviève, in Paris. This scene was obviously drawn from an Eastern model, taken from a design on some Sassanid fabric. Another is *The Prophet*, placed against a column from the cloister of Notre-Dame-des-Doms, in Avignon, from the latter half of the 12th century, in which can be detected the influence of the Royal Portal of Chartres Cathedral. The style of these works is crude, but their purity and artlessness enhance the intensity of the expressions, as will be seen in the grieving **Head of Christ 124**, in painted and gilded wood, from the first half of the 12th century, originating in Lavaudieu in the Haute-Loire, or in the grave, rustic **Virgin of Auvergne 125**, instrument of the Incarnation and the Word, from the latter half of the century.

The column-statues from the old Notre-Dame church in Corbeil-*Solomon* and, particularly, the **Queen of Sheba 126** (circa 1180-1190) -emerge as the last glimmerings of great Romanesque art, and herald the advent of the more brilliant, flexible and appealing Gothic style. This is represented in the Louvre by an array of masterpieces sufficiently complete to enable the beholder to follow its evolution from beginning to end: pieces from the major 13th-century stone-carving centers, such as the figure of Sainte Geneviève that adorned the pier of the old Paris church of which she was the patron saint; the fragment of the jube from Chartres Cathedral depicting *Saint Matthew the Evangelist* writing at an angel's dictation; 14th century figures of the Virgin and Child, such as the *Ryaux Virgin* from Lorraine and the Norman **Blanchelade Virgin 127**; and recumbent and standing effigies of sovereigns. Among the latter is a jovial figure of **Charles V 128**, which was probably intended to adorn the East Gate of the old Château du Louvre; this is one of the most remarkable pieces of medieval portrait sculpture in existence. The patronage of Duke Jean de Berry is evidenced by the Apostle's Head, attributed to Jean de Cambrai, from the church of Mehun-sur-Yèvre (Cher). The display ends with a presentation of 15th century French and Burgundian sculptures, grouped around one of the Louvre's most celebrated masterpieces, the **Tomb of Philippe Pot 129**; Philippe Pot was the Grand Seneschal of Burgundy. This piece, representing a funeral cortège, was sculpted sometime between 1477 and 1483 by an "ymagier", still unidentified, for the abbey church of Citeaux.

123 Daniel in the Lions' Den
Paris, late 11th century
Richelieu 2, Ground Floor

124 The Christ of Lavaudieu
Second quater 12th century

Richelieu 2, Ground Floor

125 Virgin of Auvergne
Second half 12th century

Richelieu 2, Ground Floor

126 The Queen of Sheba
Corbeil, circa 1180-1190

Richelieu 2, Ground Floor

During the 16th century, French sculpture underwent the influence of the Italian Renaissance, and became more delicate, subtler, less naive. Concurrently, it also became more ornamental, and blossomed forth with decorative elements from the trans-alpine repertory. Perhaps the monument that best represents its complex evolution over the first few decades is the **Saint George** 130 retable, executed in Tours for the upper chapel of the château de Gaillon by Michel Colombe, one of the last Gothic *imagiers*: this featured a new-style framework sculpted for it on the site by stone carvers from an Italian workshop. The triumph of the classical Renaissance during the second half of the century is illustrated by a series of outstanding pieces, such as Jean Goujon's bas-reliefs for the **Fountain of the Holy Innocents** 131 (1547-1549), adorned with nymphs and tritons whose sensuality is unquestionably pagan; Pierre Bontemps's funeral statue of *Admiral Philippe Chabot* (circa 1570), depicting him in a recumbent position borrowed from Etruscan statuary; Germain Pilon's **Three Graces** 132, designed for the monument that contained Henri II's heart (between 1560 and 1566), inspired by a famous antique group; and this same artist's statue of *Cardinal de Birague* kneeling in prayer (1584-1585), in which the decorative fullness of the great robe's folds foreshadows the more kinetic art of the following century.

French 17th-and 18th-century sculpture was marked by sundry successive and contrasting trends-classic, realist, mannerist, baroque-and is amply represented in the Louvre. It yielded triumphal monuments, such as the one that, in 1643, was erected near the Pont-au-Change, designed to accommodate the bronze effigies of Louis XIII, the young Louis XIV and **Queen Anne of Austria** 133, sculpted by Simon Guillain; funeral monuments, such as the elegant obelisk

127 The "Blanchelande" Virgin and Child
First third 14th century
Richelieu 2, Ground Floor

128 Charles V
(detail)
Paris, circa 1390
Richelieu 2, Ground Floor

129 Tomb of Philippe Pot
Last quarter 15th century

Richelieu 2, Ground Floor

designed circa 1663 by François Anguier for the Celestine chapel in Paris to commemorate the *Dukes of Longueville*; statues designed to adorn parks, like the four equestrian groups executed by Coysevox (1706) and Guillaume Coustou (1745) **134**, for Marly and re-erected in the courtyard of the same name, and like Puget's ardent **Milon of Crotona 135** (1682) for Versailles; pieces designed to mark a sculptor's admission into the French Academy, such as Pigalle's graceful figure of **Mercury Attaching his Heel-wing 136** (1744) and Falconnet's no less famous *Woman Bathing* (1755); statues of the *Great Men of France,* like the Caffieri's Corneille **138**, planned under the reign of Louis XVI, to adorn the Great Gallery; and, last but not least, portraits, the long series of which ends with Houdon's rich, varied work **137**.

The neoclassicism of the Revolutionary and Imperial periods illustrated by Chaudet's *Peace* was followed by a variety of trends rooted in a renewed familiarity with Antiquity and fresh interest in the Middle Ages. Passion became something to be expressed. Giraud's *Monument to his dead wife and child* is an eloquent example of this development. Sculptors did not turn to Romanticism till later. The most vigorous representatives of this trend were Pradier **139** and Rude, whose **Neapolitan Fisherman 140** was innovative in its freedom of attitude parallel to that of Barye, an exact observer of the animal world **141**. This movement is also vividly expressed in David d'Angers *Philopoemen* and Duseigneur's **Orlando Furioso 142**.

Works from foreign schools including the Netherlands, Germany, England, Spain and especially Italy **143, 144**, occupy exhibition space on the mezzanine and ground floor in the western part of the Denon Wing. Among these are two world-famous masterpieces by Michelangelo, the **Dying**

Michel COLOMBE
130 **St. George Slaying the Dragon**
Early 16th century
Richelieu 2, Ground Floor

Jean GOUJON
131 **Bas-relief from the Fountain of the Holy Innocents**
1547-1549
Richelieu 2, Ground Floor

Germain PILON
132 **Three Graces**

Circa 1560

Richelieu 2, Ground Floor

Simon GUILLAIN
133 **Anne of Austria**

1643

Richelieu 2, Ground Floor

Slave **144** and the *Rebel Slave*, sculpted from 1513 to 1515 for the tomb of Pope Julius II. They were eventually withdrawn from the monument in its final form and presented by the artist to his friend Roberto Strozzi, who offered them in homage to King Henri II of France; he in turn gave them to the High Constable de Montmorency. They remained in the latter's residence at Ecouen until 1632, when they became the property of Cardinal de Richelieu, who housed them in his château in Poitou, whence his nephew, Marshal de Richelieu, had them moved to his Paris mansion in 1749. In 1792, the statues passed into the custody of the Museum of French Monuments and from there to the Louvre, in 1794. These figures were generally assumed to be allegories of the liberal arts reduced to powerlessness by the demise of the pope, their protector.

However, the prevailing opinion today is that, like the images of captives on antique triumphal arches, they were probably designed to symbolize, on the monument's lower part, the "terrestrial counterpart of the sovereign pontiff's apotheosis, depicted in the upper part". Be that as it may, and despite their unfinished state-or perhaps even because of it-the compelling, tortured loveliness of these statues imparts intense expression, in a new manner, to Michelangelo's personal anguish at the time when he was at a height of his genius.

Guillaume Coustou
134 Horses of de Marly
1739-1745
Richelieu 2, Mezzanine

Sculptures

Jean-Baptiste PIGALLE

136 Mercury

1744

Richelieu 3, Ground Floor

Pierre PUGET

135 Milon of Crotona

1682

Richelieu 3, Mezzanine

Jean-Antoine HOUDON

137 Louise Brongniart at five years old

1777

Richelieu 3, Ground Floor

109

Jean-Jacques CAFFIERI
138 **Corneille**

1778

Richelieu 3, Ground Floor

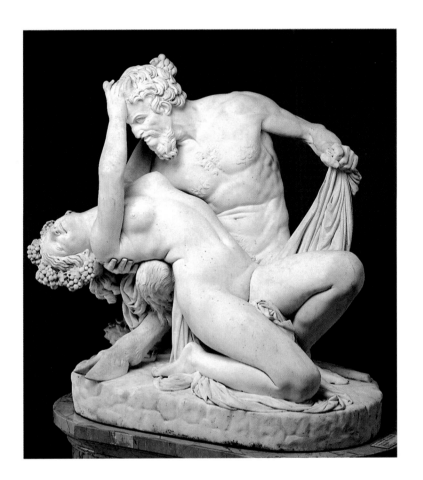

James Pradier
139 **Satyr and Bacchante**
1834

Richelieu 3, Ground Floor

François Rude
140 **The Neapolitan Fisherman**
1833

Richelieu 3, Ground Flooe

Antoine-Louis BARYE

141 Lion Crushing a Snake

1832-1835

Richelieu 3, Mezzanine

ROLAND FURIEUX

Jean-Bernard *known as* Jehan DUSEIGNEUR

142 **Orlando Furioso**

1831-1867

Richelieu 3, Mezzanine

113

MICHELANGELO

143 **The Dying Slave**

1513-1515

Denon 9, Ground Floor

Antonio CANOVA
144 Psyche and Cupid
1793
Denon 9, Ground Floor

Objets d'Art

The precious objects and items of furniture, kept in a section separate from the sculpture department since 1893, are exceptionally valuable from both the historical and artistic viewpoint. They come from the royal collections, from the former treasuries of Saint-Denis and the Order of the Holy Ghost, from the 1901 transfer to the Louvre of the former National Furniture Museum and from numerous bequests, donations and purchases down to the present time. They are displayed on the first floor of the Richelieu Wing and in the north and west wings of the Square Courtyard.

Artefacts from the Middle Ages, the Renaissance and the early 17th century are exhibited on the first floor of the Richelieu Wing. From the paleo-Christian ivories such as the *Berberini Ivory* depicting a triumphant emperor (possibly Justinian) and the Byzantine ivories including the famed mid-10th century **Harbaville Triptych 145**, which features Christ, the Virgin, St. John the Baptist, the apostles and saints, all portrayed in the precise, sophisticated style of the day, the Middle Ages are represented by works of the highest quality; among them for the Carolingian period is the outstanding **Equestrian statue of Charlemagne 146** (9th century), from the Metz Cathedral treasury, and for the Romanesque period, Limousin and Meuse-region chased-enamel pieces, such as the **Resurrection Armilla (armband) 149** (circa 1175-1180); the Gothic period is also marked by Limousin enamels (circa 1200-1210), as may be seen in *The Death of the Virgin* plate and the *Alpais Ciborium*, and by ivories like the two distinguished

13th century Parisian works: the **Descent from the Cross 148** and the enchanting *Virgin*, a model of refinement and elegance, from the treasury of the Sainte-Chapelle; these are followed by fine examples of goldsmithery, such as the gilded silver *Reliquary-triptych* from the Floreffe abbey, in Belgium (after 1254), and the *Reliquary-arms* of St. Louis of Toulouse and St. Luke, made of crystal and enamelled gilded silver in Naples.

Added to these chronological displays are certain exceptional pieces from the treasury of the abbey of Saint-Denis: a porphyry vase, known as the **Eagle of**

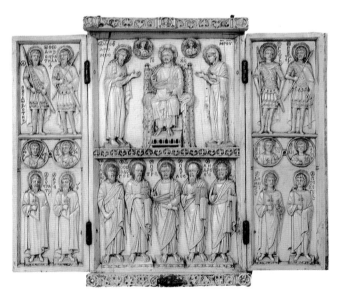

145 Harbaville Triptych
Byzantium, mid-10th century

Ivory

Richelieu 2, 1st Floor

146 The Charlemagne Statuette
9th century

Bronze

Richelieu 2, 1st Floor

147 Eagle of Suger

Mid-12th century

Porphyry and gilded silver

Richelieu 2, 1st Floor

Suger **147**, in the shape of a hieratic eagle (gilded silver), commissioned by Abbot Suger of Saint-Denis in the 12th century, or the **Virgin of Jeanne d'Evreux 150** presented to the abbey by the queen whose name it bears in 1339, and the coronation instruments or "regalia" such as the golden **Sceptre 151** topped by a statuette of Charlemagne, carved for Charles V in the 14th century.

From the end of the Middle Ages, the group of 14th and 15th century Hispano-Moresque ceramics and the *Autoportrait of Jean Fouquet* are worthy of mention; painted in gold on an enamelled copper medallion, the latter work is unique for its period, in both technique and subject.

The Renaissance collections exhibited in the new rooms of the former Ministry of Finance benefit from a display adapted to the two great tapestry cycles belonging to the department: the splendid series devoted to **Maximilian's Hunting Expeditions 153**, woven in Brussels around 1530 from designs by Bernard van Orley, and the equally famous *History of Scipio* series, made at the Gobelins factory (founded in 1662), from cartoons by Jules Romain. The majolica ensemble and bronzes from the Italian Renaissance should be mentioned, notably those by the Paduan master, Andrea Riccio, with his **Arion 152**. Works by the great Limoges enameller Leonard Limosin stand out among the painted enamels of the French Renaissance, in particular his portrait of **Anne de Montmorency 154**. Hangings and treasures from the Order of the Holy Ghost presented next to masterpieces of 16th century French goldsmithery, such as the **Helmet and shield of Charles IX 155**, in gilded and enamelled iron, complete the collections of this period.

The first floor of the north wing of the Square Courtyard, along with three

148 **Descent from the Cross**
Paris, 2nd half of the 13th century
Ivory
Richelieu 2, 1st Floor

149 **Ceremonial armband (armilla): The Resurrection**
Meuse, circa 1175-1180
Gilt and anamel on copper
Richelieu 2, 1st Floor

150 Virgin of Jeanne d'Evreux

Paris, pre-1339

Silver-gilt, translucent enamels

Richelieu 2, 1st Floor

151 Sceptre of Charles v

Before 1380

Gold, pearls, precious stones

Richelieu 2, 1st Floor

rooms in the Richelieu Wing, is devoted to decorative art in the 17th and 18th centuries. French and Italian bronzes from the late 16th and 17th centuries are on display in the Richelieu Wing, and include Barthélémy Prieur's statues of **Henri IV and Marie de Medici 156**, the works of Jean Bologne and his disciples, as well as the "Effiat Room" which presents 17th century furniture: an ebony cabinet, **bed 157** and armchairs. An outstanding piece of this period's goldsmithery is the Golden Chest thought to have belonged to Anne of Austria. The next two rooms in the Square Courtyard illustrate the art of André-Charles Boulle, the great cabinetmaker of Louis XIV who worked at the Louvre and specialized in copper and tortoiseshell marquetry with gilded bronze appliques. The David-Weill and Niarchos galleries contain masterpieces of French goldsmithery from the rococo period, notably the **Table-center of the Duc de Bourbon 159**, and from the neoclassical period. After this, a succession of rooms offer Louis XV furniture, especially the work of Charles Cressent, cabinetmaker to the regent and creator of the celebrated **Monkey Commode 160**, and a fine series of broad desks inlaid with rare woods and lacquers and covered in rococo bronzework. The great Abundance room presents an extremely complete display of woodwork and furniture from the mid-18th century. Towards 1760, the lines of furniture became more rigid in aspect, in response to the vogue for neo-classicism, while bronzework increasingly took its cue from the Greco-Roman example. This trend is chiefly represented by the work of Jean-François Deben (who made convertible furniture like the *Burgundy table* shown here), and by his disciples Jean-François Leleu and Jean-Henri Riesener. Leleu's commode for the Prince de Condé's bedroom in the Palais Bourbon is displayed against a background of Gobelins tapestries from the

Andrea RICCIO
152 Arion
Padua, circa 1500

Bronze

Richelieu 3, 1st Floor

153 The Month of August, tapestry from the "Hunts of Maximilian" series
(detail)
Brussels, circa 1530

Richelieu 3, 1st Floor

Léonard LIMOSIN
154 **The High Constable Anne de Montmorency**
1566

Enamel on copper

Richelieu 3, 1st Floor

155 **Helmet and shield of Charles IX**

Paris, circa 1572

Enamelled gilded iron

Richelieu 3, 1st Floor

same building, while Riesener was responsible for much of the collection of Marie-Antoinette's furniture held by the Louvre. Louis XVI boiseries are represented by an extensive ensemble from the Hotel de Luynes on the Rue Saint-Dominique, Paris; and the "Chinese room" contains furniture lacquered in the oriental style by Martin Carlin **161**, for the daughters of Louis XV.

The visit to the 19th century collections is temporarily divided into two parts. In the half-wing on the west side of the Square Courtyard are works from the Restoration period (*Bed of Charles X*, 1815) and from the July Monarchy (the remarkable **Grape-Harvest Bowl 164** by Froment-Meurice), while in the former Ministry of Finance, on the first floor of the wing north of the Marly Courtyard, are pieces from the late 18th century (*Bed of Madame Récamier*, 1798), and from the First Empire (**Napoleon's "Athenienne" 162** and *Empress Josephine's jewel cabinet*, 1809), along a circuit which ends with a visit to the **Rooms of Napoleon III 163**, formerly occupied by the Ministry of State.

Lastly, the department of decorative Arts counts among its prestigious treasures the famous French crown jewels, including the renownd 137-carat "Regent" diamond, acquired in 1717 by Philippe d'Orléans, who was regent during Louis XV's childhood, and which adorned the **Coronation Crown 158**, worn by Louis at this ceremony. They are displayed in the Apollo Gallery, so-called because the painter Le Brun, who in 1661 was commissioned by Louis XIV to decorate it took as his theme the Sun God, emblem of the sovereign; this theme was likewise adopted by Eugène Delacroix in 1848, when the gallery was restored by Duban, in his painting of the central section *Apollo Vanquishing the Serpent Python*.

Barthélemy PRIEUR
156 Henri IV and Marie de Medicis
Paris, circa 1610

Bronze

Richelieu 3, 1st Floor

157 Bed thought to have belonged to the Marshal d'Effiat
Mid-17th century

Richelieu 3, 1st Floor

158 Louis XV's coronation crown

Paris 1722

Denon 8, 1st Floor

Jacques RÖETTIERS

159 Table-center of the Duc de Bourbon

Paris, 1736

Silver

Sully 5, 1st Floor

123

Charles Cressent
160 Monkey Commode
Paris, circa 1735-1740

Violet and rosewood, gilded bronze

Sully 4, 1st Floor

Martin Carlin
161 Commode
Paris, circa 1780

Japanese lacquer and gilded bronze

Sully 4, 1st Floor

Martin-Guillaume BIENNAIS
162 **Napoleon I's "Athenienne" from the Tuileries**
Paris, early 19th century

Gilded bronze and yew

Richelieu 2, 1st Floor

François-Désiré FROMENT-MEURICE
164 **Grape-Harvest Bowl**
Paris, circa 1844

Agate and enamelled Silver

Sully 4, 1st Floor

125

All photography provided by : Réunion des musées nationaux
(D. Arnaudet, M. Bellot, G. Blot, M. Coursaget, C. Jean,
C. Rose, J. Schormans)
ill. 6 : © EPGL-Architecte I.M. Pei-RMN

This book was printed in January 1996 by the Mame Imprimeurs,
in Tours (France), on Job matt coated paper, 135 g

Premier dépôt légal : august 1989
Dépôt légal : January 1996
ISBN : 2-7118-3001-2
GG 20 3001